Hidden Wounds:
The Invisible Impact of Childhood Abuse on Adult Well-Being

Hidden Wounds: The Invisible Impact of Childhood Abuse on Adult Well-Being

Warrior Within

Mike Bowles

Published by Mike Bowles, 2023.

HIDDEN WOUNDS: THE INVISIBLE IMPACT OF CHILDHOOD ABUSE ON ADULT WELL-BEING

First edition. April 16, 2023.

Copyright © 2023 Mike Bowles.

ISBN: 979-8215098820

Written by Mike Bowles.

Also by Mike Bowles

Warrior Within
Warrior Within : Healing Childhood Abuse. Book 1 How Trauma
Effects the Brain,Personal Values and Affirming Self Worth
Warrior Within - Healing Childhood Abuse. Book 2 The Inner Child,
Emotional Intelligence and Boundaries
Hidden Wounds: The Invisible Impact of Childhood Abuse on Adult
Well-Being

Standalone
If Santa Was a Vampire

Contents

Chapter 1: Understanding Childhood Trauma: Types, Prevalence, and Consequences

As a survivor of childhood trauma, you are not alone. Childhood trauma refers to any experience that caused significant harm or distress to your physical or emotional well-being, such as physical or emotional abuse, neglect, sexual abuse, or exposure to domestic violence. These experiences can leave lasting wounds that impact your adult life in many ways.

It is important to recognize that the prevalence of childhood trauma is unfortunately high, with many survivors struggling with the invisible impact of their trauma. Approximately 25% of children in the United States have experienced some form of trauma, and the effects can be far-reaching and long-lasting.

As a survivor, you may have already experienced the consequences of childhood trauma, which can affect various aspects of your life, including your mental and physical health, relationships, and personal growth. Childhood trauma can increase the risk of developing mental health issues, such as depression, anxiety, and post-traumatic stress disorder (PTSD), as well as physical health problems, such as chronic pain, heart disease, and obesity. It can also affect your ability to form healthy relationships and succeed academically and professionally.

It is important to acknowledge the different types of childhood trauma and their impact on your life. Physical abuse refers to the use of physical force that results in harm or injury, while emotional abuse includes any behavior that harms your emotional well-being, such as belittling, criticizing, or insulting. Sexual abuse involves any sexual contact or behavior between an adult and a child, while neglect refers to the failure of a caregiver to provide for your basic needs, such as food, shelter, and medical care. Domestic violence involves exposure to violence between parents or other family members.

However, it is crucial to understand that healing and recovery are possible. With the right support, survivors of childhood trauma can learn to manage symptoms, build resilience, and develop healthy coping strategies. While healing from childhood trauma is not a linear process and may take time, it is important to remember that progress is possible.

One of the first steps in healing from childhood trauma is recognizing the impact that trauma has had on your life. It is common to experience feelings of shame, guilt, and self-blame, but it is important to know that these feelings are not your fault. You may need to work through these emotions and learn to identify and express your feelings in a healthy way.

Therapies like cognitive-behavioral therapy (CBT), trauma-focused therapy, and eye movement desensitization and reprocessing (EMDR) can be effective in helping you work through these emotions and develop healthy coping strategies. Building a strong support system is also crucial for healing from childhood trauma. This can include trusted friends and family members, support groups, and mental health professionals who can provide a safe and non-judgmental space for you to talk about your experiences and process your feelings.

In the following chapters, we will explore the various ways in which childhood trauma can affect adult survivors, and the different strategies and resources available for healing and recovery. By understanding the impact of childhood trauma and the pathways to healing, you can take steps towards reclaiming your life and building a brighter future. Remember that you are not alone, and healing and recovery are possible.

If you're struggling with the effects of childhood trauma, it's important to remember that seeking help is not a sign of weakness. In fact, reaching out for support takes great courage and strength. Healing from childhood trauma is a journey, but it's one that you don't have to take alone.

It's also important to recognize that the healing process may involve confronting difficult emotions and memories, which can be challenging and overwhelming at times. However, with the right support and resources, you can learn to manage these emotions in a safe and healthy way.

As you begin your journey towards healing, it may also be helpful to remember that recovery is not a destination. Rather, it's a lifelong process of growth and self-discovery. While the effects of childhood trauma can be long-lasting, they do not have to define you or limit your potential. With time, patience, and persistence, you can learn to overcome the invisible impact of childhood trauma and live a fulfilling and meaningful life.

In the following chapters, we will explore different aspects of the invisible impact of childhood trauma, including how it affects mental and physical health, relationships, and personal growth. We will also provide strategies and resources for healing and recovery, including various therapies, self-care practices, and support networks.

Remember, you are not alone. Childhood trauma may be an invisible wound, but it's one that can be healed with the right support and resources. You deserve to live a life that is free from the burden of your past, and with the right tools and mindset, you can learn to thrive in the present and future.

Chapter 2: The Ripple Effect: How Childhood Abuse Affects Adult Relationships

When we experience childhood trauma, it can leave deep emotional scars that affect every aspect of our lives, including our relationships with others. Childhood abuse can cause us to feel a sense of mistrust and fear, making it difficult to form close connections with others. This can lead to feelings of loneliness, isolation, and a lack of belonging.

As someone who has experienced childhood abuse, it's important to understand that the impact of this trauma on your relationships may not always be immediately apparent. You may find yourself struggling to connect with others, or you may find that your relationships are fraught with conflict and tension.

One common way that childhood abuse can affect adult relationships is through patterns of attachment. Attachment patterns are developed early in life and are influenced by the way we were cared for as children. When we experience abuse or neglect in childhood, it can lead to insecure attachment styles that make it difficult to trust others and form healthy relationships.

Childhood abuse can also affect different types of relationships in unique ways. For example, if you experienced emotional or physical abuse at the hands of a parent or caregiver, it may be difficult to form healthy boundaries with others in your adult life. You may find yourself either pushing people away out of fear of being hurt, or becoming too clingy and reliant on others for validation and support.

In romantic relationships, childhood abuse can lead to feelings of insecurity, jealousy, and fear of abandonment. You may find yourself constantly seeking validation and reassurance from your partner, or becoming overly clingy and possessive. Alternatively, you may avoid close relationships altogether out of fear of being hurt or rejected.

Friendships can also be impacted by childhood abuse. You may struggle to form close connections with others, or find yourself becoming too dependent on friends for emotional support. You may also find it difficult to trust others or open up about your past experiences, leading to feelings of isolation and disconnection.

Family dynamics can also be impacted by childhood abuse. If you experienced abuse from a family member, it may be difficult to trust and connect with other family members in your adult life. You may feel a sense of loyalty to the abuser or feel guilt and shame for speaking out against them. This can lead to a breakdown in family relationships and feelings of isolation and alienation.

In addition, childhood abuse can impact our ability to regulate our emotions and cope with stress. This can lead to difficulties in managing conflict and navigating complex social situations. You may find yourself becoming easily overwhelmed or triggered by situations that remind you of your past trauma, leading to unhealthy coping mechanisms such as substance abuse or self-harm.

It's important to understand that the impact of childhood abuse on our relationships is complex and multifaceted. However, with the right support and resources, it's possible to heal from these wounds and form healthy, fulfilling relationships. This may involve seeking therapy or counseling, joining a support group, or practicing self-care and mindfulness techniques.

Remember, you are not defined by your past experiences. You have the power to take control of your life and build healthy, fulfilling relationships with others. It may not be easy, but it is possible. In the following chapters, we will provide you with the tools and resources you need to heal from the invisible wounds of your past and create a bright and hopeful future.

Chapter 3 Living in Fear: The Lasting Impact of Childhood Abuse on Mental Health

When we experience childhood abuse, it can leave a lasting impact on our mental health. The trauma and stress of abuse can lead to a range of mental health issues, including anxiety, depression, PTSD, and other mood disorders.

As someone who has experienced childhood abuse, it's important to understand that the impact of this trauma on your mental health may not always be immediately apparent. You may find yourself struggling with symptoms such as anxiety and depression, but may not connect these issues to your past experiences of abuse.

One common mental health issue experienced by survivors of childhood abuse is anxiety. This can take many different forms, from generalized anxiety and worry to panic attacks and phobias. Survivors may also experience social anxiety and a fear of interacting with others, or a fear of abandonment and rejection.

Depression is another common mental health issue experienced by survivors of childhood abuse. This can manifest in many different ways, from a lack of motivation and energy to persistent feelings of sadness and hopelessness. Survivors may also experience suicidal thoughts or engage in self-harm as a coping mechanism.

PTSD, or post-traumatic stress disorder, is another mental health issue commonly experienced by survivors of childhood abuse. This can lead to intrusive thoughts and memories of the abuse, as well as nightmares and flashbacks. Survivors may also experience hyperarousal and a constant state of fear and anxiety. Hyperarousal is a common symptom experienced by individuals who have been exposed to trauma, including childhood abuse. Hyperarousal refers to an excessive or heightened state of alertness, arousal, and sensitivity to stimuli in the environment. There are different types of hyperarousal, including:

1. Hypervigilance: Hypervigilance refers to an intense state of vigilance and awareness of one's surroundings, often accompanied by an exaggerated startle response, irritability, and difficulty sleeping.
2. Emotional reactivity: Emotional reactivity involves intense and frequent emotional responses to stimuli that may be perceived as neutral or minor by others. For example, an individual may become extremely upset or angry over a minor criticism or comment.
3. Sleep disturbances: Individuals experiencing hyperarousal may have difficulty falling or staying asleep, or may experience nightmares or other sleep disturbances.
4. Physical symptoms: Hyperarousal can also manifest in physical symptoms such as muscle tension, headaches, and gastrointestinal problems.

It's important to understand that these mental health issues are a natural response to the trauma of childhood abuse. You are not weak or flawed for experiencing these symptoms. Rather, they are a sign that your mind and body have been impacted by a traumatic experience.

In order to heal from these mental health issues, it's important to seek professional help. Therapy and counseling can provide a safe and supportive space to process your trauma and develop coping skills for managing anxiety, depression, and PTSD. Medication may also be a helpful tool for managing symptoms.

In addition to professional help, there are also self-care practices that can be helpful in managing mental health issues related to childhood abuse. This may include mindfulness practices such as meditation and yoga, as well as engaging in activities that bring you joy and fulfillment.

It's important to acknowledge that the impact of childhood abuse on mental health is complex and can vary from person to person. Some survivors may experience symptoms of anxiety or depression immediately following the abuse, while others may not experience these symptoms until years later.

It's also important to understand that the impact of childhood abuse on mental health can be exacerbated by other life stressors. For example, survivors may experience additional stress and trauma related to financial instability, job loss, or relationship issues. These stressors can trigger symptoms of anxiety, depression, and PTSD.

As someone who has experienced childhood abuse, it's important to be kind and compassionate with yourself. The healing process can be long and challenging, but with the right support and resources, it's possible to overcome these challenges and build a happy and healthy life.

Remember, you are not defined by your past experiences. You are a strong and resilient individual who has survived a traumatic experience. By seeking professional help and engaging in self-care practices, you can learn to manage your mental health issues and build a fulfilling life. In the following chapters, we will provide you with the tools and resources you need to overcome the lasting impact of childhood abuse on your mental health.

Lost in Translation: The Language of Abuse and Its Lasting Effects

One of the lasting effects of childhood abuse is the way it impacts our relationship with language. For survivors, the language of abuse can feel like a foreign language, one that is filled with triggers and painful memories. The words and phrases used by abusers can become a source of anxiety and trauma, making it difficult to communicate effectively in our daily lives.

For example, a survivor of physical abuse may struggle to use words such as "hit" or "beat" in everyday conversation without feeling triggered.

Similarly, a survivor of emotional abuse may have difficulty expressing their emotions or communicating their needs, as they may have learned to hide their true feelings as a coping mechanism.

The language of abuse can also impact our self-talk and internal dialogue. Survivors may have a harsh and critical inner voice, one that echoes the negative messages they heard from their abusers. This can lead to feelings of low self-worth and self-doubt, making it difficult to trust oneself and others.

It's important to understand that these challenges with language are a normal response to the trauma of childhood abuse. You are not alone in struggling to communicate and process the language of abuse.

One way to overcome these challenges is to seek professional help. A therapist or counselor can provide a safe and supportive space to explore the impact of the language of abuse on your life, and develop coping skills for managing triggers and anxiety related to language.

In addition to professional help, there are also self-care practices that can be helpful in managing the impact of the language of abuse on your life. This may include journaling or creative writing as a way to process and express your emotions, or practicing mindfulness to develop a greater awareness of your inner dialogue.

Remember, you are not defined by the language of abuse. It's possible to reclaim language and develop a healthy relationship with communication. By seeking professional help and engaging in self-care practices, you can learn to manage the impact of the language of abuse on your life and build a brighter future.

Breaking the Cycle: Healing from Childhood Abuse and Preventing Intergenerational Trauma

As someone who has experienced childhood abuse, you know all too well the lasting impact it can have on your life. But what you may not realize is that the effects of childhood abuse can continue to impact generations to come, creating a cycle of trauma that can be difficult to break.

Breaking the cycle of abuse requires a commitment to healing and a willingness to seek help. It also requires an understanding of the factors that contribute to the cycle of abuse, such as the impact of trauma on brain development and the way that abuse can impact attachment and relationships.

For example, if you grew up in a household where you witnessed domestic violence, you may have learned that aggression and violence are acceptable ways to resolve conflict. As a result, you may be more likely to enter into relationships with abusers or to become an abuser yourself.

Healing from childhood abuse is a complex process that involves both individual and collective efforts. For many survivors, individual efforts may include seeking therapy or counseling to address the impact of trauma, developing healthy coping strategies, and building a strong support system. It may also involve setting boundaries with family members who perpetuate the cycle of abuse or seeking out new role models who can provide guidance and support.

Collective efforts to prevent intergenerational trauma may involve advocacy work to raise awareness about the impact of childhood abuse and to push for policies that prioritize prevention and intervention. This could include supporting programs that provide resources to families who are at risk of abuse or holding abusers accountable for their actions.

Ultimately, breaking the cycle of abuse is about creating a world where all children can grow up feeling safe, loved, and supported. It's about recognizing that childhood abuse is not inevitable and that we all have a role to play in creating a more just and equitable society.

Chapter 4: Reclaiming Your Voice: Overcoming the Shame and Silence of Childhood Abuse

Childhood abuse can leave survivors feeling alone, helpless, and powerless. Often, these feelings are intensified by shame and self-blame, leading many survivors to remain silent about their experiences.

Reclaiming your voice after childhood abuse is a crucial step in the healing process. It involves breaking through the shame and silence that often accompany abuse and speaking out about your experiences. This can be an incredibly difficult and painful process, but it is also one that can be incredibly empowering.

It's important to understand that speaking out about your abuse is a personal decision, and there is no right or wrong way to do so. It can be challenging to confront painful memories and emotions, and it's okay to take your time to build up the strength and courage to share your story. Remember that you are not alone, and there is support available to help you through this process.

One way to reclaim your voice after childhood abuse is to find a safe and supportive community. This can be a group of other survivors, a therapist, or a supportive friend or family member. It's important to find someone who you feel comfortable talking to and who can provide you with the support and validation that you need.

In addition to finding a supportive community, engaging in creative expression can also help you to reclaim your voice. Creative expression can take many forms, such as art, writing, or music, and can be a powerful tool for healing. It can allow you to express emotions and experiences that may be difficult to put into words and can provide a sense of release and catharsis.

Another important aspect of reclaiming your voice is learning to set healthy boundaries. Childhood abuse can make it challenging to understand what boundaries are and how to establish them. Setting boundaries can help you to feel more in control of your life and can help you to maintain a sense of safety and security. It's essential to take the time to identify your own personal boundaries and to communicate them to others.

setting boundaries is an essential aspect of reclaiming your voice after childhood abuse. It involves identifying your own personal limits and communicating them to others in a clear and assertive manner. Here are some steps to help you set healthy boundaries:

1. Identify your boundaries: Take the time to think about what makes you feel safe and comfortable. This may include physical boundaries (e.g., personal space), emotional boundaries (e.g., not tolerating verbal abuse), or social boundaries (e.g., not engaging in activities that make you uncomfortable). Once you've identified your boundaries, write them down and keep them somewhere accessible.

2. Communicate your boundaries: It's important to communicate your boundaries to others in a clear and assertive manner. This can be challenging, especially if you're used to being passive or accommodating. Remember that it's okay to say no and to set limits on what you're comfortable with. Practice using "I" statements, such as "I feel uncomfortable when you speak to me like that" or "I need some space right now."

3. Enforce your boundaries: It's essential to enforce your boundaries consistently. This means following through on what you've communicated and not tolerating behavior that violates your limits. It's important to be firm but also respectful when enforcing your boundaries. Remember that it's not your responsibility to manage other people's reactions, and it's okay to walk away from situations that are not respectful of your boundaries.

4. Be flexible: Boundaries are not set in stone, and they can

change over time. It's important to be flexible and to reassess your boundaries as needed. It's also essential to recognize that other people may have different boundaries, and it's important to respect their limits as well.

Setting boundaries can be challenging, especially if you've experienced childhood abuse. It's important to be patient with yourself and to seek support from a therapist or a supportive community if you're struggling. Remember that setting boundaries is an important step towards reclaiming your voice and building a sense of self-worth and empowerment.

Remember that reclaiming your voice is a process, and it may take time and patience to feel comfortable speaking out about your experiences. But know that your voice matters, and by speaking out, you are not only empowering yourself but also helping to create a world where childhood abuse is no longer tolerated.

Chapter 5 "Coping Strategies: How Survivors of Childhood Abuse Learn to Cope."

Survivors of childhood abuse often develop coping strategies to manage the emotional and physical effects of trauma. Coping strategies can be helpful in managing symptoms like anxiety, depression, and flashbacks, and can also help survivors feel a sense of control over their lives. Here are some examples of coping strategies that survivors of childhood abuse may use:

Mindfulness:

1. Mindfulness involves paying attention to the present moment without judgment. Survivors of childhood abuse may find mindfulness practices like deep breathing or meditation helpful in managing anxiety and stress. Mindfulness can also help survivors stay grounded in the present moment, rather than being overwhelmed by memories of the past.Breathing exercises are a great way to reduce stress and anxiety. Here are some examples of breathing exercises:

• Deep breathing: Take a deep breath in through your nose, hold it for a few seconds, and then slowly exhale through your mouth. Repeat this several times until you feel more relaxed.

• Box breathing: Inhale for four counts, hold for four counts, exhale for four counts, and then hold for four counts. Repeat this cycle several times.

• Belly breathing: Place one hand on your chest and the other on your belly. Breathe in through your nose, feeling your belly expand, and then exhale through your mouth, feeling your belly contract.

• Alternate nostril breathing: Place your right thumb over your right nostril and inhale through your left nostril. Then, use your right ring finger to close your left nostril and exhale through your right nostril. Repeat this cycle, switching nostrils with each inhale and exhale.

- 4-7-8 breathing: Breathe in through your nose for four counts, hold your breath for seven counts, and then exhale through your mouth for eight counts.

Remember to always breathe slowly and deeply, and focus on your breath to help calm your mind and reduce stress.

Creative expression:

1. Creative expression can be a powerful way for survivors of childhood abuse to process their emotions and memories. This may include activities like writing, drawing, or music. Creative expression can also help survivors feel a sense of control over their experiences, and can provide a way to communicate feelings that may be difficult to express in words.

Self-care:

1. Self-care involves prioritizing your own physical and emotional needs. Survivors of childhood abuse may find self-care practices like taking a warm bath, going for a walk in nature, or spending time with loved ones helpful in managing stress and anxiety. Self-care can also be an important reminder that survivors are worthy of care and attention, despite messages they may have received in the past that they are not.

It's important to remember that coping strategies are unique to each individual and may change over time. What works for one survivor may not work for another, and it's important to find strategies that feel authentic and meaningful to you. Survivors of childhood abuse may also benefit from working with a therapist or support group to develop and refine coping strategies that work for their specific needs.

Chapter 6: The Invisibility of Trauma - Challenges to Disclosure and Recovery

The impact of childhood abuse can be invisible to others and can be difficult for survivors to articulate. This can make it challenging for survivors to seek help and disclose their experiences to others. In this chapter, we will explore some of the challenges that survivors face when it comes to disclosing their experiences and seeking recovery.

Shame and self-blame are common emotions that many survivors of childhood abuse experience. Survivors may feel that the abuse was their fault or that they somehow deserved it, leading to a sense of guilt and self-blame. This can make it challenging for them to disclose their experiences to others, as they may fear judgment or rejection.Guilt and self-blame can manifest in many different ways for survivors of childhood abuse. They may feel that the abuse was their fault or that they somehow deserved it, leading to a sense of guilt and self-blame. This can result in feelings of worthlessness, shame, and a distorted sense of self. Survivors may also blame themselves for not being able to prevent or stop the abuse, even if they were unable to do so due to the power dynamics at play.

Guilt and self-blame can also lead survivors to engage in self-destructive behaviors, such as substance abuse or self-harm. They may feel that they deserve punishment for the abuse they experienced or that they need to numb the pain and trauma they are experiencing.

Survivors may also struggle with trust and intimacy in their relationships, as they may feel that they are unworthy of love and care. They may feel that they are inherently flawed or damaged, and that they are not deserving of healthy relationships. This can make it challenging for survivors to form meaningful connections with others and can lead to feelings of loneliness and isolation.

Fear of retribution is another challenge that survivors of childhood abuse may face when it comes to disclosure. Survivors may fear retaliation or retribution from their abuser if they disclose the abuse, particularly if the abuser is a family member or someone in a position of authority. This fear can be particularly acute if the abuse is ongoing or if the survivor is still in contact with the abuser.

Lack of understanding from others is also a significant challenge that survivors of childhood abuse may encounter when they disclose their experiences. Many people may not fully appreciate the long-term effects of childhood trauma, which can lead to a lack of empathy and understanding from others. This can be particularly true if the abuse occurred in childhood, as many people may believe that survivors should have "gotten over it" or "moved on" by now.

Difficulty accessing resources is another challenge that many survivors of childhood abuse face when it comes to seeking help and recovery. Survivors may encounter barriers to accessing resources like therapy or support groups, particularly if they lack financial resources or live in areas with limited access to mental health services.

Despite these challenges, it is possible for survivors of childhood abuse to heal and recover. Seeking help from a therapist or support group can be an important first step, as can finding supportive friends and family members who can provide emotional support. It's important for survivors to remember that healing is a process and that there is no "right" way to recover - what works for one survivor may not work for another. With time, patience, and compassion, it is possible to overcome the challenges of trauma and move towards a place of healing and growth.

Chapter 7: From Victim to Survivor: The Journey of Healing from Childhood Abuse

Healing from childhood abuse can be a long and challenging journey. It requires a great deal of courage, strength, and resilience, as well as a willingness to confront and work through the pain and trauma of the past. However, with the right support and resources, it is possible for survivors to move from being a victim to becoming a survivor and even thriving in their lives.

The journey of healing typically begins with acknowledging the abuse and its impact on one's life. This can be a difficult and painful process, as survivors may have spent years denying or minimizing the abuse in order to cope. However, it is a crucial first step towards healing and can provide a foundation for the work to come.Starting the journey towards healing from childhood abuse can be a difficult and emotional process. Many survivors, like myself, struggle to come to terms with the lasting impact that abuse has had on their lives. It often takes a significant event or realization to finally acknowledge the abuse and begin the journey towards healing.

For me, it wasn't until I hit a low point in my life that I was able to confront the abuse I had experienced. I found myself struggling with anxiety, depression, and feelings of worthlessness that I couldn't seem to shake. It was only after seeking help from a therapist that I began to understand the role that childhood abuse had played in these struggles.

From there, I began to take small but meaningful steps towards healing. I sought out resources and support, both online and in-person, from other survivors who could relate to my experiences. I also made a conscious effort to practice self-care, prioritizing my mental and emotional wellbeing in ways that felt meaningful to me.

Through this journey, I learned that healing is not a linear process. There were times when I felt stuck or like I was moving backwards, but I came to understand that this was all part of the journey. Healing from childhood abuse requires patience, compassion, and a willingness to confront difficult emotions and experiences.

Ultimately, the journey towards healing from childhood abuse is unique to each survivor. But by taking those first steps towards acknowledging the abuse and seeking out support, survivors can begin to reclaim their lives and move towards a place of healing and empowerment.

Therapy can be an important part of the healing journey, providing a safe and supportive space to explore and process the impact of the abuse. A therapist can help survivors to identify and work through negative patterns of thinking and behavior, as well as develop coping skills to manage the emotional and psychological fallout of the abuse.

Other forms of support can also be beneficial, such as joining a support group or connecting with other survivors who can offer empathy, validation, and understanding. It's important for survivors to know that they are not alone and that healing is possible.

The journey of healing may also involve confronting and challenging beliefs and attitudes that were shaped by the abuse. This may include negative self-talk, feelings of shame or guilt, and difficulty trusting others. Survivors may need to relearn healthy coping strategies and ways of relating to themselves and others that were undermined by the abuse.

As survivors progress in their healing journey, they may begin to shift their identity from being a victim to becoming a survivor. This can involve a sense of empowerment and a greater sense of agency in one's life. Survivors may begin to set boundaries and prioritize self-care, as well as engage in activities that bring joy and fulfillment.

Ultimately, the journey of healing from childhood abuse is a unique and individual process. It may involve setbacks and challenges along the way, but with support and a commitment to self-care, survivors can move towards a place of healing and growth.

Chapter 8: The Role of Support Systems in the Recovery Process

Recovering from childhood abuse is a journey that can be challenging and overwhelming at times. It can be difficult to know where to start or how to cope with the many complex emotions that arise. That's why having a support system is so crucial to the healing process.

For me, my support system consisted of a few close friends and family members who I trusted and felt comfortable opening up to about my experiences. They provided a safe and non-judgmental space where I could share my struggles and feel heard and validated. Their support gave me the strength and courage to continue on my healing journey, even when it felt like too much to handle.

But support can come in many forms, and what works for one person may not work for another. Some survivors find solace in support groups or therapy, while others turn to creative outlets like art or writing to express their emotions. The important thing is to find what works for you and to seek out support that feels genuine and non-judgmental.

It's also important to recognize that building a support system can take time and effort. It may require reaching out to new people or organizations and being vulnerable in ways that feel uncomfortable. But by taking these steps, survivors can begin to build a network of people and resources that can help them navigate the challenges of healing from childhood abuse.

Building a support system from scratch can be a daunting task, especially for survivors of childhood abuse who may have trust issues and fear of vulnerability. However, it's a crucial step in the healing process. Here are some steps to consider:

1. Identify potential sources of support: Think about people in your life who you feel comfortable with and trust, such as friends, family members, co-workers, or even acquaintances

who have expressed empathy and understanding.

2. Be honest and clear about your needs: Let your potential support system know what you need from them. It could be as simple as someone to listen, someone to accompany you to therapy sessions, or someone to check in with you regularly.

3. Seek professional support: Consider reaching out to a therapist or counselor who specializes in trauma and abuse. They can provide guidance on building a support system and help you navigate any challenges that may arise.

4. Join support groups: There are many support groups available for survivors of childhood abuse, both online and in-person. These groups can provide a safe space for you to connect with others who have gone through similar experiences.

5. Practice self-care: Building a support system takes time and effort, so it's important to take care of yourself along the way. Make sure to prioritize self-care activities such as exercise, meditation, and hobbies that bring you joy.

Remember, building a support system is a process, and it may take time to find the right people and resources. Be patient with yourself and trust that with time, you will find the support you need to heal and thrive.

Support systems can also play a crucial role in addressing the shame and self-blame that many survivors experience. By receiving validation and empathy from others, survivors can begin to internalize the message that the abuse was not their fault and that they deserve to heal and move forward.

In short, the role of support systems in the recovery process cannot be overstated. Whether it's a friend, family member, therapist, support group, or creative outlet, finding and cultivating supportive relationships and resources can make all the difference in the healing journey.

Chapter 9: Trapped in Time: The Impact of Childhood Abuse on Adult Identity

Childhood abuse can have a profound impact on an individual's sense of self and identity. Many survivors of abuse struggle with feelings of shame, low self-worth, and a distorted sense of self, which can impact their relationships, work, and overall well-being. This chapter explores the ways in which childhood abuse can shape an individual's identity, as well as the challenges and opportunities for healing and growth.

The Formation of Identity

Identity is a complex and multifaceted concept that encompasses an individual's sense of self, personality, values, beliefs, and relationships. It is shaped by a range of factors, including genetics, upbringing, culture, and life experiences. Childhood abuse can have a significant impact on the formation of identity, as it can shape an individual's perceptions of themselves and the world around them.

Childhood abuse can lead to a distorted sense of self, as survivors may struggle to differentiate their own experiences and emotions from those of their abuser. This can lead to feelings of confusion, self-doubt, and a lack of trust in their own perceptions. Survivors may also struggle with shame and guilt, as they may feel responsible for the abuse or believe that they somehow deserved it.

In addition, childhood abuse can impact an individual's relationships with others, which can further impact their sense of identity. Survivors may struggle to trust others, fear abandonment, or struggle with attachment and intimacy issues. These difficulties can make it challenging to form meaningful connections and may further contribute to a distorted sense of self.

Challenges to Identity

The impact of childhood abuse on identity can manifest in a range of ways. Survivors may struggle with a range of challenges, including:

1. Low self-worth and self-esteem: Survivors of childhood abuse may struggle with feelings of shame, guilt, and low self-worth. They may believe that they are unworthy of love and respect, which can impact their relationships and overall well-being.
2. Emotional dysregulation: Childhood abuse can impact an individual's ability to regulate their emotions, leading to difficulties with anger, anxiety, and depression. Survivors may struggle to express their emotions or may experience intense emotional reactions to triggers.
3. Self-destructive behaviors: Survivors of childhood abuse may engage in self-destructive behaviors as a way of coping with their trauma. This can include substance abuse, self-harm, or other risky behaviors.
4. Dissociation: Survivors may experience dissociation, which involves a sense of disconnection from themselves or their surroundings. This can be a coping mechanism to manage overwhelming emotions or trauma.

Healing and Growth

While childhood abuse can have a significant impact on an individual's sense of identity, healing and growth are possible. The journey towards healing and growth can involve a range of strategies, including therapy, self-reflection, and building supportive relationships.

1. Therapy: Therapy can be a powerful tool for survivors of childhood abuse, as it can help individuals process their trauma, develop coping strategies, and build resilience. Therapists may use a range of approaches, including cognitive-behavioral therapy, trauma-focused therapy, or other evidence-based treatments.
2. Self-reflection: Survivors may benefit from engaging in self-reflection and introspection, which can involve journaling, meditation, or other mindfulness practices. These activities can

help individuals connect with their own thoughts and emotions and develop a greater sense of self-awareness.

3. Supportive relationships: Building supportive relationships with friends, family, or a support group can be a critical component of the healing process. These relationships can provide a sense of validation, support, and encouragement, which can help survivors develop a more positive sense of self.

The impact of childhood abuse on adult identity is a complex and multifaceted issue that can manifest in various ways. For many survivors of childhood abuse, their traumatic experiences can leave an indelible mark on their identity and sense of self, making it difficult to form healthy relationships, establish boundaries, and trust others.

One way in which childhood abuse can impact adult identity is through the formation of negative self-beliefs and self-talk. Survivors of childhood abuse may internalize the negative messages they received from their abuser, leading them to believe that they are unworthy, unlovable, or inherently flawed. This negative self-talk can become so ingrained that it can be difficult to challenge, even when presented with evidence to the contrary.

Another way in which childhood abuse can impact adult identity is through the development of maladaptive coping mechanisms. In an effort to protect themselves from further harm, survivors of childhood abuse may engage in behaviors that provide a temporary sense of relief but ultimately reinforce negative self-beliefs and hinder their ability to form healthy relationships. These behaviors can include substance abuse, self-harm, disordered eating, and compulsive behaviors.

For some survivors of childhood abuse, the trauma they experienced may lead them to dissociate from their sense of self entirely. This can result in feelings of numbness, disconnection, and a lack of purpose or direction in life. Survivors may struggle to connect with their emotions, form meaningful relationships, or find a sense of belonging in the world around them.

Despite the challenges that survivors of childhood abuse may face in terms of their identity and sense of self, there is hope for healing and recovery. Through therapy, support groups, and other forms of treatment, survivors can learn to challenge their negative self-talk, develop healthy coping mechanisms, and rebuild their sense of self.

It is important to acknowledge that the journey of healing and recovery from childhood abuse is a process that takes time and effort. Survivors may experience setbacks, and progress may feel slow at times. However, with the right support and resources, survivors can find a sense of purpose, meaning, and belonging in their lives, and develop a more positive and resilient sense of self.

Chapter 10: Untangling the Web of Shame and Guilt: Overcoming the Emotional Toll of Childhood Abuse

Childhood abuse can leave deep emotional wounds, causing survivors to experience overwhelming feelings of shame and guilt. These emotions can have a lasting impact on their mental health and ability to form healthy relationships. Overcoming these feelings requires a lot of work and a deep understanding of the root causes of shame and guilt.

Shame and guilt often go hand in hand for survivors of childhood abuse. Shame is a complex emotion that is often experienced by individuals who have been victims of childhood abuse. It is an intense feeling of humiliation or disgrace that can be triggered by a range of situations or experiences. For survivors of childhood abuse, shame can be deeply ingrained in their sense of self and identity, leading to a pervasive feeling of being flawed, inadequate, or unworthy.

Shame can manifest in various ways, including self-blame, self-criticism, and a sense of worthlessness. Survivors may feel ashamed of what happened to them, as if they somehow brought it upon themselves or are to blame for their abuse. They may also feel ashamed of their own reactions to the abuse, such as feeling helpless, scared, or powerless. In addition, survivors may feel ashamed of the impact the abuse has had on their lives, such as struggling with mental health issues, substance abuse, or difficulties in relationships.

Shame can be a major barrier to healing and recovery from childhood abuse. It can prevent survivors from seeking help or support, as they may feel too ashamed or embarrassed to talk about their experiences. Shame can also fuel feelings of isolation and loneliness, as survivors may feel that they are the only ones who have gone through such experiences. Therefore, it is important to address shame as part of the healing process, to help survivors learn to understand and manage their feelings in a more constructive way.

Guilt is a feeling of responsibility or remorse for something one has done wrong. Survivors of childhood abuse often feel intense shame and guilt, even when they are not responsible for the abuse that occurred.

It is important to recognize that shame and guilt are common reactions to trauma and abuse. These emotions are not a reflection of the survivor's worth or character. Rather, they are a response to the abuse and trauma that was inflicted upon them. Healing from childhood abuse requires understanding the nature of shame and guilt and developing strategies to cope with them.

One approach to overcoming shame and guilt is to challenge negative self-talk. Negative self-talk is the internal dialogue that we have with ourselves that reinforces feelings of shame and guilt. It is important for survivors to identify and challenge these negative thoughts, replacing them with positive and affirming messages. This can help survivors to break the cycle of shame and guilt and build self-esteem.Negative self-talk can be a harmful habit that can stem from childhood abuse. It can manifest in a person's life by causing self-doubt, low self-esteem, and feelings of unworthiness. Here are some practical ways to overcome negative self-talk:

1. Identify the negative self-talk: The first step is to identify when negative self-talk is happening. It can be helpful to write down negative thoughts as they occur so that patterns can be recognized and addressed.

2. Challenge the negative thoughts: Once negative self-talk is identified, challenge the thoughts with evidence that contradicts them. For example, if a person thinks, "I'm not good enough," they can challenge that thought by reminding themselves of their accomplishments or positive feedback they have received.

3. Practice self-compassion: Negative self-talk can be a result of

harsh self-judgment. Practicing self-compassion involves treating oneself with the same kindness, concern, and understanding as one would a good friend. This can involve positive self-talk, self-care, and being gentle with oneself.

4. Surround oneself with positive influences: It can be helpful to surround oneself with positive influences such as supportive friends and family members, uplifting media, and positive affirmations.

5. Seek therapy: Childhood abuse can cause deep-rooted issues that may require professional help to address. Seeking therapy can provide a safe space to explore and work through negative self-talk and the underlying causes.

It's important to remember that overcoming negative self-talk is a process that takes time and effort. Consistency and persistence are key to making progress towards a more positive and self-affirming mindset.

Another approach is to seek out professional support. Therapists and counselors can provide a safe and supportive environment for survivors to work through feelings of shame and guilt. They can also help survivors to develop coping strategies to manage these emotions as they arise.

It is important to recognize that healing from childhood abuse is a journey, and there is no one-size-fits-all approach. Survivors may need to try different strategies and techniques to find what works best for them. It is also important to remember that healing is not linear, and setbacks may occur. But with patience, perseverance, and support, survivors can overcome the emotional toll of childhood abuse and reclaim their lives.

Chapter 11: Sexual Abuse: Trauma, Stigma, and Recovery

Sexual abuse is a type of childhood trauma that can have a lasting impact on an individual's mental health, relationships, and overall well-being. Unfortunately, sexual abuse survivors often face stigma and shame that can prevent them from seeking the help they need to heal. This chapter will explore the stigma surrounding sexual abuse and provide strategies for survivors to recover and reclaim their lives.

The Stigma of Sexual Abuse

Sexual abuse is often stigmatized by society, leading survivors to feel ashamed and isolated. Survivors may also experience victim blaming, where they are blamed for the abuse that occurred. Victim blaming within families can be a particularly hurtful and damaging aspect of the aftermath of childhood abuse. Oftentimes, family members cannot accept responsibility for the abuse that occurred or are ashamed that it happened within their family, so they may try to shift the blame onto the victim. This can manifest in a number of ways, including questioning the victim's behavior or actions leading up to the abuse, suggesting that they are lying or exaggerating, or even outright denying that the abuse occurred. These actions can leave the victim feeling isolated, unsupported, and further traumatized. It is important for families to take responsibility for their role in allowing abuse to occur, to provide support and validation to the victim, and to take active steps towards healing and recovery as a family unit. This can lead to feelings of self-blame and further perpetuate the stigma surrounding sexual abuse. It is important to recognize that sexual abuse is never the fault of the survivor and that seeking help is a courageous and necessary step in the healing process.

Recovery from Sexual Abuse

Recovering from sexual abuse can be a long and challenging process, but it is possible. Therapy, support groups, and self-care practices can all be helpful in the recovery process. It is important for survivors to work with a therapist who specializes in trauma and sexual abuse to develop a personalized treatment plan.

Here are some practical strategies that survivors can use to support their recovery:

1. Practice self-care: Self-care can include activities such as

exercise, meditation, spending time with loved ones, or engaging in hobbies. It is important to prioritize self-care and make time for activities that bring joy and relaxation.

2. Join a support group: Support groups can provide a sense of community and understanding among survivors. It can be helpful to connect with others who have had similar experiences and share coping strategies.

3. Challenge negative thoughts: Negative thoughts and self-talk can be a common symptom of trauma. It can be helpful to challenge these thoughts by asking yourself if they are based in reality and reframing them in a more positive light.

4. Set boundaries: Setting boundaries is an important part of self-care and can help survivors feel more in control. It is okay to say no to activities or people that feel triggering or uncomfortable.

Conclusion

Sexual abuse is a traumatic experience that can have a lasting impact on survivors. Stigma and shame can prevent survivors from seeking help and can further perpetuate the negative effects of the abuse. However, recovery is possible, and survivors can reclaim their lives with the help of therapy, support groups, and self-care practices. It is important to prioritize self-care and seek professional help to support the healing process.

Chapter 12: The Intersection of Childhood Abuse and Substance Abuse

Childhood abuse can have a profound impact on an individual's emotional, psychological, and physical health. One of the most common ways that survivors of childhood abuse attempt to cope with the pain and trauma they have experienced is through substance abuse. According to the National Child Traumatic Stress Network, survivors of childhood abuse are at a significantly higher risk for developing substance abuse disorders than those who have not experienced abuse.

The relationship between childhood abuse and substance abuse is complex, and it can be challenging for survivors to break the cycle of addiction without proper support and treatment. Substance abuse can also exacerbate the symptoms of PTSD, depression, and anxiety that often accompany childhood abuse. Survivors of childhood abuse may turn to drugs or alcohol to numb their emotions, ease the pain of their traumatic memories, or simply to escape their reality.

In addition to substance abuse, survivors of childhood abuse are also at an increased risk of suicidal ideation and suicide attempts. Studies have found that childhood abuse survivors who develop substance abuse disorders are more likely to attempt suicide than those without substance abuse disorders. The trauma and emotional pain that accompany childhood abuse can be overwhelming, and survivors may feel that there is no other way to escape their pain.

The stigma surrounding substance abuse and mental health issues can also be a significant barrier for survivors seeking help. Family members, friends, and even healthcare professionals may be quick to judge survivors who struggle with addiction, and may not understand the complex interplay between childhood abuse and substance abuse. It is essential that survivors of childhood abuse are provided with non-judgmental support and access to appropriate resources to help them overcome their addiction and heal from their trauma.

According to the Substance Abuse and Mental Health Services Administration, trauma-informed care is an evidence-based approach to treatment that takes into account the impact of childhood abuse on an individual's overall health and well-being. This approach involves creating a safe, non-judgmental environment where survivors can feel comfortable discussing their experiences and accessing the support they need to recover. Trauma-informed care recognizes that substance abuse is often a symptom of deeper emotional pain and seeks to address the underlying trauma that drives addiction.

In conclusion, the intersection of childhood abuse and substance abuse is a complex issue that requires a compassionate and evidence-based approach to treatment. Survivors of childhood abuse who struggle with addiction must be provided with the support they need to break the cycle of addiction and heal from their trauma. By addressing the underlying trauma that drives addiction and providing non-judgmental support, survivors can begin to rebuild their lives and find hope and healing on their journey to recovery.

Chapter 13: Breaking the Cycle: Healing from Inter-generational Trauma

Childhood abuse and trauma can have a profound impact not only on the survivors but also on their future generations. Inter-generational trauma refers to the transfer of trauma and its effects from one generation to the next. This can occur through various means such as direct exposure to trauma, witnessing the effects of trauma on a parent or caregiver, or through learned behaviors and coping mechanisms. For example, a child may experience trauma due to domestic violence in their home, which can impact their mental and emotional well-being. This trauma may then be passed down to their own children if they struggle to manage their trauma-related symptoms and engage in harmful coping mechanisms, such as substance abuse or violence. Another example could be a family who has experienced historical trauma, such as the forced removal and relocation of Indigenous children from their families, which can impact future generations through loss of culture, disconnection from family, and a continued cycle of trauma. Breaking the cycle of inter-generational trauma requires awareness, healing, and supportive interventions to prevent the continued transfer of trauma to future generations. Research has shown that the effects of trauma can be passed down through families, resulting in a cycle of abuse and trauma that can span multiple generations. Breaking this cycle requires a deep understanding of the root causes of inter-generational trauma, as well as a commitment to healing and change.

One of the key ways to break the cycle of inter-generational trauma is to acknowledge and address the trauma that has been passed down from previous generations. This involves acknowledging the pain and suffering that has been experienced by both the survivors and their ancestors, and working to heal and transform the trauma.

It's important to recognize that healing from inter-generational trauma is a complex and ongoing process that requires patience, compassion, and support. It can involve individual therapy, group therapy, family therapy, and other forms of support. In addition, it may require working through difficult emotions and memories, including anger, shame, and guilt, in order to break free from the patterns of behavior and thinking that have been passed down through generations.

One of the challenges of healing from inter-generational trauma is the sense of isolation and shame that can come with acknowledging the trauma that has been experienced. Many survivors may feel that they are alone in their experiences or that they are somehow to blame for what has happened. It's important to remember that the effects of inter-generational trauma are not the fault of any individual, and that healing requires a collective effort that involves both individuals and communities.

Breaking the cycle of inter-generational trauma also involves developing healthy coping mechanisms and relationships that support healing and growth. This can include developing a strong sense of self, cultivating healthy boundaries, and building supportive relationships with family, friends, and community members. It may also involve exploring spiritual or cultural practices that provide a sense of connection and healing.

According to research, individuals who have experienced childhood trauma and abuse are at higher risk for addiction and suicidal ideation. Therefore, it's important to address any substance abuse issues and suicidal thoughts in the healing process. Seeking professional help, such as counseling or addiction treatment, can be an important step in breaking the cycle of inter-generational trauma.

In conclusion, breaking the cycle of inter-generational trauma requires a deep commitment to healing and transformation. It involves acknowledging and addressing the trauma that has been passed down through generations, developing healthy coping mechanisms and relationships, and seeking professional help when needed. While the healing journey can be difficult and complex, it's important to remember that it's never too late to start the journey and that healing is possible.

Chapter 14: Overcoming the Stigma of Mental Illness and Childhood Abuse: Breaking Barriers to Treatment

The stigma surrounding mental illness can be a significant barrier for survivors of childhood abuse seeking treatment. Many individuals may feel ashamed or embarrassed to seek help, fearing that they will be judged or ostracized by others. Additionally, mental illness related to childhood abuse can often go unrecognized or misdiagnosed, further exacerbating the problem.

One common mental illness that can result from childhood abuse is post-traumatic stress disorder (PTSD). PTSD can cause flashbacks, nightmares, and other symptoms that make it difficult to function in daily life.

Emotional PTSD (Post Traumatic Stress Disorder) is a mental health condition that is triggered by a traumatic event, such as childhood abuse. Emotional PTSD occurs when the person has persistent and distressing symptoms, such as intrusive memories or flashbacks, avoidance of reminders of the trauma, negative changes in thoughts and mood, and increased arousal and reactivity.

Emotional PTSD can also be characterized by emotional dysregulation, which involves difficulty in managing emotions, extreme emotional reactions, and intense mood swings. People with emotional PTSD may experience feelings of anxiety, depression, and anger, and may also have difficulty forming and maintaining relationships due to emotional numbness and detachment.

Treatment for emotional PTSD often involves therapy, such as cognitive behavioral therapy (CBT) or eye movement desensitization and reprocessing (EMDR), which can help individuals process and cope with traumatic experiences and emotions. Medications, such as antidepressants or anti-anxiety medications, may also be used in conjunction with therapy to alleviate symptoms of emotional PTSD.

Survivors may also experience depression, anxiety, or substance abuse as a result of the trauma they endured.

Another response to childhood abuse is dissociation, which involves a disconnection from one's thoughts, feelings, or memories as a way of coping with overwhelming experiences. This can manifest in a variety of ways, such as feeling detached from reality or one's own emotions, or experiencing gaps in memory surrounding the abuse. Dissociation is a psychological defense mechanism in which a person mentally separates themselves from their surroundings, feelings, or experiences. This disconnection can range from mild detachment to more severe forms, such as dissociative disorders. Dissociation is often a coping mechanism that helps a person deal with overwhelming or traumatic experiences, such as childhood abuse. People report dissociation as feeling like a detachment from reality, as if they are observing themselves from the outside or as if the world around them is unreal or foggy. It can also involve feeling emotionally numb or disconnected from their own thoughts and feelings. Some individuals may describe it as feeling like they are in a dream-like state or as if their body is not their own. Symptoms can range from mild to severe and can last for short or prolonged periods of time. Treatment options for dissociation typically involve therapy, such as cognitive-behavioral therapy or dialectical behavior therapy, and medication may also be used in some cases.

Treatment for dissociation often involves therapy, particularly trauma-focused therapy. This type of therapy can help a person work through their traumatic experiences in a safe and supportive environment, which can help to reduce dissociation symptoms. Other treatment options may include medication to manage anxiety or depression, as well as relaxation techniques like meditation or yoga.

It's important for survivors to know that seeking treatment is not a sign of weakness, but rather a courageous step towards healing. Therapy, medication, and support groups can all be effective forms of treatment for mental illness related to childhood abuse. However, it's essential that survivors work with trained professionals who understand the complexities of trauma and are equipped to provide appropriate care.

Breaking the stigma surrounding mental illness and childhood abuse requires education and awareness. By speaking out about their experiences and advocating for better treatment options, survivors can help reduce the shame and isolation that often accompany mental illness. With the right support and resources, survivors of childhood abuse can find hope and healing on their journey towards recovery.

The stigma surrounding mental health and childhood abuse can create significant barriers to seeking and accessing treatment. Many survivors of childhood abuse may feel ashamed or embarrassed to seek help, and may also face social stigma and discrimination if they do. Additionally, access to mental health services may be limited or difficult to navigate, particularly for those who are low-income or from marginalized communities. Here are some examples of barriers to treatment and ways to overcome them:

1. Shame and embarrassment: Survivors of childhood abuse may feel ashamed or embarrassed to seek help, particularly if they have internalized blame or stigma surrounding their experiences. Overcoming these feelings may involve recognizing that seeking help is a sign of strength and resilience, and that there is no shame in needing support.

2. Lack of knowledge: Many survivors of childhood abuse may not be aware of the resources available to them or may not understand the link between their experiences and their mental health. Increasing knowledge and awareness can involve doing research, reaching out to trusted sources such as therapists or support groups, and talking openly about mental health and abuse.

3. Financial barriers: Access to mental health services can be

limited for those who are low-income or underinsured. However, there are many resources available for those who cannot afford therapy or treatment, including sliding-scale clinics, free support groups, and online resources.

4. Cultural barriers: For some survivors of childhood abuse, cultural or religious beliefs may create barriers to seeking help. It is important to recognize that seeking support is not a betrayal of one's cultural or religious beliefs, and that many religious or cultural communities have resources and support available.

5. Trauma-related symptoms: Survivors of childhood abuse may experience a range of trauma-related symptoms, including dissociation, flashbacks, and anxiety, which can make seeking help feel overwhelming or impossible. It is important to recognize that these symptoms are a normal response to trauma and that treatment can help to alleviate them.

Overcoming these barriers requires a combination of personal and systemic changes. It involves challenging stigma and stereotypes surrounding mental health and childhood abuse, advocating for increased access to mental health services, and creating safe spaces for survivors to seek support and healing. By breaking down these barriers, we can help to ensure that all survivors of childhood abuse are able to access the care and support they need to heal and thrive.

Chapter 15: Hidden Wounds of Childhood Abuse on Physical Health

Childhood abuse has a profound impact not only on mental health but also on physical health. Survivors of childhood abuse are more likely to experience a range of physical health problems, including chronic pain, autoimmune disorders, heart disease, and gastrointestinal disorders. This is due to the fact that childhood abuse can disrupt the body's stress response system, leading to chronic inflammation and other physiological changes that increase the risk of disease.

1. Chronic pain: Childhood abuse can cause physical injuries that result in chronic pain. Additionally, the experience of chronic stress and trauma can cause a heightened sensitivity to pain, making it more difficult for survivors to manage pain.

2. Autoimmune disorders: Childhood abuse can also lead to an increased risk of autoimmune disorders, such as lupus, rheumatoid arthritis, and multiple sclerosis. This is due to the fact that chronic stress and trauma can suppress the immune system, leading to an overactive immune response that attacks healthy tissue.

3. Heart disease: Childhood abuse can also increase the risk of heart disease. Studies have shown that individuals who experienced childhood abuse are more likely to have high blood pressure, elevated cholesterol levels, and other risk factors for heart disease.

It is important for survivors of childhood abuse to prioritize their physical health as well as their mental health. This may involve working with a healthcare provider to manage chronic health conditions, adopting healthy lifestyle habits such as regular exercise and a balanced diet, and seeking out support from friends, family, or a therapist. With the right care and support, survivors of childhood abuse can take steps towards healing and improving their overall health and well-being.

Childhood sexual abuse can have severe long-term effects on the genitalia, particularly in cases of repeated or violent abuse. The physical trauma inflicted on the genitals during abuse can lead to lasting damage, such as scarring, tearing, or even complete loss of function. In addition to the physical damage, survivors may experience ongoing pain, discomfort, or difficulty with sexual functioning. This can lead to feelings of shame, embarrassment, and a reluctance to seek medical care or engage in sexual activity. Survivors may also be at increased risk for sexually transmitted infections, as well as chronic conditions such as pelvic inflammatory disease or cervical cancer. The long-term impact of genital abuse can be devastating, and survivors may require ongoing medical and emotional support to manage their symptoms and regain a sense of control over their bodies.

Chapter 16: Breaking the Silence: Advocating for Survivors of Childhood Abuse

Childhood abuse is a pervasive issue that affects millions of people worldwide. It is important to acknowledge the prevalence of this issue and to advocate for the rights and needs of survivors. Advocacy for survivors of childhood abuse involves creating awareness about the issue, promoting prevention strategies, and supporting survivors in their healing journey.

One of the most critical aspects of advocating for survivors is to break the silence surrounding childhood abuse. Many survivors feel shame and embarrassment about their experiences and may not feel comfortable discussing them. It is essential to create a safe and non-judgmental environment for survivors to share their stories and seek support.

Advocacy efforts can include promoting education and awareness about childhood abuse, including prevention strategies such as educating parents and children about body safety and consent. It can also involve working with lawmakers to ensure that adequate resources are available for survivors, such as trauma-informed therapy, medical care, and legal assistance.

Advocacy can also involve supporting survivors in their journey to healing. This can include creating support groups, connecting survivors with resources, and advocating for changes in the legal system to hold abusers accountable. Advocates can also promote self-care strategies for survivors, such as mindfulness, exercise, and journaling.

It is important to note that advocacy efforts should prioritize the voices and experiences of survivors themselves. Survivors of childhood abuse should be at the forefront of advocacy efforts, and their needs and concerns should be taken seriously.

There are several organizations and resources available for individuals interested in advocating for survivors of childhood abuse. These include national organizations such as the National Children's Alliance and Darkness to Light, as well as local organizations and support groups.

In conclusion, advocating for survivors of childhood abuse is a critical aspect of promoting healing and preventing future abuse. Breaking the silence surrounding childhood abuse, promoting prevention strategies, and supporting survivors in their journey to healing are essential components of advocacy efforts. By working together, we can create a safer and more supportive environment for survivors of childhood abuse.

Advocating for survivors of childhood abuse is crucial in breaking the silence surrounding this issue. One important way to advocate for survivors is to support organizations that provide resources and services for survivors. Many non-profit organizations focus on advocacy, prevention, and support services for survivors of childhood abuse. These organizations often rely on donations and volunteers to fund and run their programs.

Another way to advocate for survivors is to raise awareness about the issue of childhood abuse. This can be done by participating in events, such as marches or rallies, that promote awareness and advocate for policy changes that will protect children and provide resources for survivors. Additionally, sharing information on social media, hosting educational events, and engaging in conversations with friends and family about the issue can help raise awareness and break the silence.

It's also important to hold institutions and individuals accountable for their actions or lack of action in cases of childhood abuse. This includes reporting instances of abuse to law enforcement and advocating for changes in laws and policies that protect survivors and hold perpetrators accountable.

Advocating for survivors of childhood abuse can be a challenging and emotionally taxing process, but it's important work that can make a significant difference in the lives of survivors. By supporting organizations that provide resources and services, raising awareness, and holding institutions accountable, we can work towards breaking the silence and creating a safer world for children.

Advocating for survivors of childhood abuse has made significant differences in various contexts. One notable example is the Me Too movement, which started as a hashtag on social media and evolved into a global movement that has brought to light the prevalence of sexual abuse and harassment. The movement has encouraged many survivors to come forward and share their stories, leading to increased awareness, accountability, and changes in policies and laws. Additionally, advocacy groups like RAINN (Rape, Abuse & Incest National Network) and Darkness to Light have made significant strides in providing support, resources, and education to survivors and their communities. Through their efforts, more survivors have access to services like hotlines, counseling, and advocacy, and more individuals are trained to recognize and report abuse. Furthermore, advocacy efforts have led to changes in laws and policies, such as extending the statute of limitations for reporting abuse and implementing mandatory reporting requirements for certain professionals.

Advocacy efforts have led to changes in laws related to childhood abuse in many countries around the world. Here are a few examples:

1. United States: The Child Abuse Prevention and Treatment Act (CAPTA) was passed in 1974, which established a federal framework for reporting and responding to child abuse and neglect. Many states have also passed laws extending the statute of limitations for survivors of childhood abuse to file civil lawsuits against their abusers.

2. United Kingdom: The Children Act 1989 was passed in the UK, which placed a duty on local authorities to investigate and intervene in cases of child abuse. In 2015, the UK government also passed the Modern Slavery Act, which includes provisions to protect children from trafficking and exploitation.

3. Australia: The Royal Commission into Institutional Responses to Child Sexual Abuse was established in 2013, which investigated the response of institutions such as schools, churches, and sports clubs to allegations of child abuse. The commission made several recommendations for legal and institutional reforms, many of which have been implemented.

Advocacy efforts have also led to increased awareness of childhood abuse and its impacts, as well as increased funding for support services for survivors.

Chapter 17: Cultivating Resilience: How to Thrive Despite Childhood Abuse

Childhood abuse can have a devastating impact on a person's life. However, it is possible to cultivate resilience and thrive despite the trauma. Resilience is the ability to adapt to difficult situations and bounce back from adversity. Here are some ways to cultivate resilience:

1. Seek support: Building a support system can provide a sense of safety and comfort. This can include friends, family, therapists, or support groups.
2. Practice self-care: Self-care can include a variety of activities, such as exercise, meditation, or hobbies that bring joy. Taking care of one's physical and emotional health is essential to building resilience.
3. Find meaning and purpose: Finding meaning and purpose in life can help individuals overcome adversity and develop a sense of resilience. This can involve pursuing a passion, volunteering, or finding a meaningful career.
4. Reframe negative thoughts: Negative thoughts can be a barrier to resilience. Reframing negative thoughts into positive ones can help individuals cultivate a more positive outlook on life.
5. Practice forgiveness: Forgiving oneself and others can be a powerful tool in building resilience. Letting go of anger and resentment can create space for healing and growth.

Examples of resilience in survivors of childhood abuse can include finding a supportive community, pursuing education or a career, and creating healthy relationships with family and loved ones. Resilience can be cultivated through various methods, and each person's journey will be unique. It takes time, patience, and effort, but with the right tools and support, individuals can learn to thrive despite childhood abuse.

It is possible to heal from the effects of childhood abuse and go on to lead a fulfilling life. While the road to recovery can be long and challenging, it is worth the effort. The healing process begins with recognizing and acknowledging the impact of the abuse on one's life. It may also involve seeking professional support, such as therapy or counseling, to work through the trauma and learn healthy coping mechanisms.

It is important to note that healing from childhood abuse does not mean forgetting or denying what happened. Instead, it involves finding ways to live with the trauma and move forward in a positive direction. This may involve developing a strong support network of friends, family, and professionals who can offer encouragement and guidance.

Many survivors of childhood abuse find that cultivating resilience is an essential part of their healing journey. This may involve focusing on self-care, such as regular exercise, a healthy diet, and good sleep hygiene. It may also involve finding ways to express emotions and creativity through activities such as art, music, or writing.

Ultimately, the journey of healing from childhood abuse is unique to each individual. It may involve ups and downs, setbacks and successes, but with perseverance, self-compassion, and the support of others, it is possible to move beyond the pain and lead a fulfilling life.

There are several examples of famous people who have overcome childhood abuse and gone on to lead successful and fulfilling lives.

One example is Oprah Winfrey, who was physically and sexually abused as a child. Despite these traumatic experiences, she went on to become a successful media mogul and philanthropist. In addition to her successful career, she has also been open about her experiences with abuse and has used her platform to advocate for survivors and raise awareness about the issue.

Another example is Maya Angelou, who was also a survivor of childhood sexual abuse. She went on to become a celebrated writer and poet, known for her powerful and inspiring works. She was also an advocate for social justice and worked tirelessly to promote equality and fight against discrimination.

Actor and comedian Jim Carrey is another example of someone who has overcome childhood abuse. Carrey has spoken publicly about his experiences with poverty and emotional abuse as a child, and how these experiences shaped him as a person. Despite these challenges, he went on to become one of the most successful and beloved actors of his generation, known for his comedic talent and impressive range as a performer.

These examples show that while childhood abuse can be a devastating experience, it is possible to heal and go on to live a fulfilling and successful life. It takes courage, resilience, and a willingness to seek help and support, but with the right resources and mindset, survivors can overcome the trauma of their past and thrive in the present.

Chapter 18: When the Abuser Is a Parent: Navigating Complex Family Dynamics

Childhood abuse is often perpetrated by a close family member, such as a parent or caregiver, making the healing journey even more complicated. When the abuser is a parent, survivors may struggle with feelings of betrayal, confusion, and a sense of loss. The parent-child relationship is one of the most fundamental relationships in a person's life, and childhood abuse can shatter the trust that is essential to that relationship.

In cases where the abuse is sexual in nature, the survivor may struggle with feelings of guilt, shame, and a sense of responsibility for the abuse. The abuser may use their position of power and authority to manipulate the survivor and keep them silent, adding an additional layer of complexity to the already challenging healing journey.

Survivors may feel torn between a desire to maintain a relationship with their parent and the need to protect themselves from further harm. This can be especially difficult when the abuser denies the abuse or refuses to take responsibility for their actions. Family members may also pressure the survivor to forgive and forget, or even blame the survivor for causing the family to be torn apart.

Navigating these complex family dynamics requires a great deal of support and self-care. Survivors may need to set clear boundaries with their abuser and other family members, and prioritize their own well-being above preserving the family unit. This can be especially challenging when there are siblings involved, and the survivor may feel responsible for protecting them as well. That being said sometimes there is also a need to cut off a family member.

Cutting off a family member after experiencing childhood abuse can be a difficult and complex decision, but it may be necessary for the survivor's healing and well-being. There are many reasons why a survivor may choose to cut off contact with a family member who was an abuser, including:

1. Safety: In some cases, the abuser may still pose a threat to the survivor's safety or the safety of their loved ones. This may be especially true if the abuse was recent or ongoing.
2. Lack of accountability: If the abuser has not taken responsibility for their actions or shown any remorse, the survivor may feel that there is no possibility for reconciliation or healing within the relationship.
3. Boundary-setting: Cutting off contact with the abuser can be a way for the survivor to establish healthy boundaries and take control of their life.
4. Emotional healing: It may be difficult for the survivor to heal and move on from the abuse if they are still in contact with the abuser or other family members who are not supportive.

While cutting off contact with an abuser can be a difficult decision, it can also lead to positive outcomes for the survivor. For example, it can help them to:

1. Feel empowered: Cutting off contact can be a way for the survivor to take control of their life and feel empowered.
2. Protect themselves: By cutting off contact, the survivor can protect themselves from further abuse and trauma.
3. Focus on healing: Removing the abuser from their life can help the survivor to focus on their healing and emotional well-being.
4. Build healthy relationships: Cutting off contact can create space for the survivor to build healthy relationships with supportive people who can help them on their healing journey.

It's important to note that cutting off contact with an abuser is not the only solution and may not be the best solution for everyone. Each survivor's situation is unique, and there may be other ways to address the complex family dynamics that result from childhood abuse. Counseling and therapy can be helpful in exploring these options and making a decision that is right for the survivor.

In cases of sexual abuse, survivors may also need to navigate the legal system and the possibility of criminal charges against the abuser. This can be a difficult and emotionally draining process, but it can also be empowering to hold the abuser accountable for their actions.

It is important for survivors to remember that they are not alone, and there are resources available to help them navigate these complex family dynamics. Support groups, therapy, and advocacy organizations can provide a safe space for survivors to share their experiences, learn coping strategies, and connect with others who have been through similar experiences.

Breaking the cycle of abuse within a family is possible, but it requires a commitment to healing and a willingness to confront difficult truths. It may also require a level of distance from the abusive parent or family members, in order to prioritize one's own healing and well-being. While this can be a difficult and painful process, it can also be incredibly empowering and liberating to break free from the cycle of abuse and live a life free from the shadow of childhood trauma.

Chapter 19: Healing through Self-Care: Nurturing the Body, Mind, and Soul

Healing from childhood abuse is a long and difficult journey. It requires a lot of patience, courage, and support. It can be easy to get lost in the pain and trauma, but it is essential to remember that self-care is crucial to the healing process. Self-care is not selfish; it is a necessary step in the journey of healing.

Taking care of yourself means treating yourself with love and kindness. It means prioritizing your physical, mental, and emotional health. One way to do this is by taking care of your body. This can include eating a healthy diet, getting enough sleep, and exercising regularly. It's also essential to listen to your body and give it what it needs, whether it's rest, relaxation, or something else entirely.

Taking care of your mind is just as important as taking care of your body. One way to do this is by practicing mindfulness, such as meditation or deep breathing exercises. It can also mean seeing a therapist or counselor who can help you work through the trauma and emotions that come with childhood abuse.

Taking care of your soul is essential too. It's about connecting with your inner self and doing things that make you happy. This can mean finding a creative outlet, such as painting or writing, or spending time in nature. It's about doing things that bring you joy and fulfillment.

As someone who has been through childhood abuse, I understand the difficulty of prioritizing self-care. It can be challenging to feel worthy of taking care of yourself when you've been made to feel unworthy by your abuser. However, it's important to remember that you deserve to be taken care of and that self-care is not a luxury, but a necessity.

Self-care can also be a powerful tool in the healing process. By taking care of yourself, you are showing yourself that you are worthy of love and kindness. It can help you feel more empowered and in control of your life. It can also help you cope with the difficult emotions and memories that come with healing from childhood abuse.

In conclusion, self-care is an essential part of the healing journey. It's about taking care of your body, mind, and soul and prioritizing your physical, mental, and emotional health. It can be challenging to prioritize self-care, but it's essential to remember that you deserve to be taken care of. Self-care is not a luxury; it's a necessary step in the journey of healing from childhood abuse.

Chapter 20: Reclaiming Power and Control: Moving Beyond the Trauma of Childhood Abuse

Reclaiming power and control is an important step in the healing journey for survivors of childhood abuse. Abuse can leave survivors feeling helpless and powerless, often leading to feelings of shame, guilt, and self-blame. Reclaiming power and control involves breaking free from the cycle of abuse, taking responsibility for one's own healing, and creating a life of purpose and meaning.

One of the key ways to reclaim power and control is through self-awareness. It is important for survivors to understand how their past experiences have shaped their thoughts, behaviors, and relationships. This self-awareness can help survivors identify patterns of behavior and make conscious choices to change them.

Another important step in reclaiming power and control is to set healthy boundaries.Setting boundaries is an essential part of healing from childhood abuse and reclaiming power and control over one's life. Here are some practical steps to set boundaries:

1. Identify your values and needs: Before setting boundaries, it is essential to understand what values and needs are essential to you. Take some time to reflect on what you value most in your

life and what your needs are in your relationships.

2. Communicate your boundaries clearly: Once you know your values and needs, communicate your boundaries clearly and assertively. Be specific about what behaviors are acceptable or not acceptable to you.

3. Use "I" statements: Use "I" statements when communicating your boundaries to avoid blaming or accusing the other person. For example, "I feel uncomfortable when you raise your voice at me."

4. Be consistent: Consistency is key when it comes to setting boundaries. Stick to your boundaries, and do not waiver when the other person tries to push back or test your limits.

5. Practice self-care: Setting boundaries can be challenging and emotional, so it is essential to practice self-care to manage any stress or anxiety that may arise. Take care of yourself by engaging in activities that bring you joy and relaxation.

Remember, setting boundaries is about taking care of yourself and your well-being. It is okay to say no and prioritize your needs, and doing so can help you heal and move beyond the trauma of childhood abuse.

Survivors of childhood abuse often struggle with boundary-setting, which can lead to difficulties in relationships and a sense of being taken advantage of. Learning to set healthy boundaries is an important part of reclaiming power and control, as it allows survivors to protect themselves from further harm and to create a sense of safety.

Forgiveness is also an important part of reclaiming power and control. Forgiveness does not mean forgetting or excusing the abuse, but rather, it is a way for survivors to release the anger and resentment that can hold them back from healing. Forgiveness is a complex and emotional process that can have both positive and negative effects on survivors of childhood abuse. It is important to understand the potential pros and cons of forgiveness before embarking on this journey.

Pros:

1. Healing and Closure: Forgiveness can be a powerful tool for healing emotional wounds and finding closure. It can provide a sense of relief and release from the pain and anger associated with the abuse.
2. Improved Relationships: Forgiveness can also improve relationships, especially with the abuser or others who may have been involved in the abuse. It can lead to greater understanding, empathy, and compassion.
3. Personal Growth: Forgiveness can be an opportunity for personal growth and development. It can help individuals develop resilience, empathy, and a sense of inner strength.

Cons:

1. Pressure and Obligation: Society often places pressure on survivors to forgive, even when they are not ready or willing to do so. This can create feelings of obligation and guilt, which can further exacerbate the trauma.
2. Re-victimization: Forgiveness can also open the door for re-victimization, especially if the abuser is still present in the survivor's life. It can create a power dynamic that can be exploited by the abuser.
3. Invalidating the Pain: Finally, forgiveness can sometimes be seen as invalidating the pain and suffering of survivors. It can suggest that what happened was not that bad, or that the survivor should just "move on" and forget about it.

In conclusion, forgiveness can be a powerful tool for healing and personal growth, but it should not be taken lightly or forced upon survivors. It is important to understand the potential pros and cons of forgiveness and to make a decision that is right for the individual survivor. Ultimately, the survivor's well-being and healing should be the priority in any decision about forgiveness.

Finally, finding purpose and meaning in life can be a powerful way to reclaim power and control. Survivors of childhood abuse often struggle with feelings of worthlessness and low self-esteem, but finding a sense of purpose and meaning can help to counteract these feelings. This can involve finding a career that is fulfilling, pursuing hobbies and interests, volunteering, or giving back to others. Finding one's purpose in life is a journey that can take time and effort. Here are some steps that can be helpful:

1. Self-reflection: Take some time to reflect on your interests, values, and passions. What activities make you feel energized and fulfilled? What kind of work or activities do you find meaningful?
2. Exploration: Explore different opportunities and activities that align with your interests and values. This can involve trying out new hobbies, taking classes, volunteering, or seeking out new work experiences.
3. Networking: Connect with others who share your interests and passions. Attend events, join clubs or organizations, and build relationships with people who can provide support, advice, and inspiration.
4. Experimentation: Be open to trying new things and taking risks. Sometimes, it takes trying different experiences to discover what truly resonates with you and what you want to pursue.
5. Reflection and adjustment: Take time to reflect on your experiences and adjust your goals and plans as needed. It's okay to change direction and adjust your course based on what you learn about yourself and what you find fulfilling.

Ultimately, finding your purpose involves exploring your interests and passions, taking risks and trying new things, and being open to self-reflection and adjustment along the way. It can be a challenging process, but the rewards of discovering your purpose can be profound and life-changing

Reclaiming power and control is not an easy process, but it is a necessary one for survivors of childhood abuse to move beyond their trauma and create a fulfilling and meaningful life. It requires self-awareness, boundary-setting, forgiveness, and finding purpose and meaning in life. With the right support and resources, survivors can reclaim their power and control and move forward with hope and healing.

Also by Mike Bowles

Warrior Within
Warrior Within : Healing Childhood Abuse. Book 1 How Trauma
Effects the Brain,Personal Values and Affirming Self Worth
Warrior Within - Healing Childhood Abuse. Book 2 The Inner Child,
Emotional Intelligence and Boundaries
Hidden Wounds: The Invisible Impact of Childhood Abuse on Adult
Well-Being

Standalone
If Santa Was a Vampire